JE 18 '21.

D0287281

Manda
Compa

Chinese Graded Reader

Breakthrough Level: 150 Characters

小明

Xiǎo Míng

Xiao Ming,
Boy Sherlock

by John Pasden and Jared Turner

Mind Spark Press LLC

SHANGHAI

Springdale Public Library
405 S. Pleasant
Springdale, AR 72764

Published by Mind Spark Press LLC

Shanghai, China

Mandarin Companion is a trademark of Mind Spark Press LLC.

Copyright © Mind Spark Press LLC, 2019

For information about educational or bulk purchases, please contact
Mind Spark Press at business@mandarincompanion.com.

Instructor and learner resources and traditional Chinese editions of
the Mandarin Companion series are available
at www.MandarinCompanion.com.

First paperback print edition 2019

Library of Congress Cataloging-in-Publication Data
Pasden, John.

Xiao Ming, Boy Sherlock : Mandarin Companion Graded Readers: Level 0,
Simplified Chinese Edition / John Pasden and Jared Turner; [edited by] John
Pasden, Chen Shishuang, Li Jiong, Ma Lihua

2nd paperback edition, April 2020.

Shanghai, China / Salt Lake City, UT: Mind Spark Press LLC, 2019

Library of Congress Control Number: 2019951286
ISBN: 9781941875575 (Paperback)
ISBN: 9781941875599 (Paperback/traditional ch)
ISBN: 9781941875582 (ebook)
ISBN: 9781941875605 (ebook/traditional ch)
MCID: SFH20200421T151307JT

All rights reserved; no part of this publication may be reproduced,
stored in a retrieval system, transmitted in any form, or by any means,
electronic, mechanical, photocopying, recording, or otherwise,
without the prior written permission of the publishers.

What level is right for me?

If you are able to comfortably read this book without looking up lots of words, then this book is likely at your level. It is ideal to have at most only one unknown word or character for every 40-50 words or characters that are read.

Once you are able to read fluidly and quickly without interruption you are ready for the next level. Even if you are able to understand all of the words in the book, we recommend that readers build fluidity and reading speed before moving to higher levels.

How will this help my Chinese?

Reading extensively in a language you are learning is one of the most effective ways to build fluency. However, the key is to read at a high level of comprehension. Reading at the appropriate level in Chinese will increase your speed of character recognition, help you to acquire vocabulary faster, teach you to naturally learn grammar, and train your brain to think in Chinese. It also makes learning Chinese more fun and enjoyable. You will experience the sense of accomplishment and confidence that only comes from reading entire books in Chinese.

Mandarin Companion Graded Readers

Now you can read books in Chinese that are fun and help accelerate language learning. Every book in the Mandarin Companion series is carefully written to use characters, words, and grammar that a learner is likely to know.

The Mandarin Companion Leveling System has been meticulously developed through an in-depth analysis of textbooks, education programs and natural Chinese language. Every story is written in a simple style that is fun and easy to understand so you improve with each book.

Mandarin Companion Breakthrough Level

The Breakthrough Level is intended for Chinese learners who have obtained a low elementary or novice level of Chinese. Most students will be able to approach this book after one year of traditional formal study, depending on the learner and program. In creating this story, we have carefully balanced the need for level-appropriate simplicity against the needs of the story's plot.

The Breakthrough Level is written using a core set of 150 characters, a subset of the 300 characters used in Mandarin Companion Level 1. This ensures that the vocabulary will be limited to simple, everyday words, composed of characters that the learner is most likely to know. Any new characters used outside of the 150 Breakthrough Level characters are exclusively borrowed from the Level 1 character set, meaning that with each new story, the reader is systematically building toward Level 1.

Key words that the reader is not likely to know are added gradually over the course of the story accompanied by a numbered footnote for each instance. Pinyin and an English definition are provided at the bottom of the page for the first instance of each key word, and a complete glossary is provided at the back of the book. All proper nouns have been underlined to help the reader distinguish between names and other words.

Extensive Reading

After years of studying Chinese, many people ask, "why can't I become fluent in Chinese?" Fluency can only happen when the language enters our "comfort zone." This comfort comes after significant exposure to and experience with the language. The more times you meet a word, phrase, or grammar point the more readily it will enter your comfort zone.

In the world of language research, experts agree that learners can acquire new vocabulary through reading only if the overall text can be understood. Decades of research indicate that if we know approximately 98% of the words in a book, we can comfortably "pick up" the 2% that is unfamiliar. Reading at this 98% comprehension level is referred to as "extensive reading."

Research in extensive reading has shown that it accelerates vocabulary learning and helps the learner to naturally understand grammar. Perhaps most importantly, it trains the brain to automatically recognize familiar language, thereby freeing up mental energy to focus on meaning and ideas. As they build reading speed and fluency, learners will move from reading "word by word" to processing "chunks of language." A defining feature is that it's less painful than the "intensive reading" commonly used in textbooks. In fact, extensive reading can be downright fun.

Graded Readers

Graded readers are the best books for learners to "extensively" read. Research has taught us that learners need to "encounter" a word 10-30 times before truly learning it, and often many more times for particularly complicated or abstract words. Graded readers are appropriate for learners because the language is controlled and simplified, as opposed to the language in native texts, which is inevitably difficult and often demotivating. Reading extensively with graded readers allows learners to bring together all of the language they have studied and absorb how the words naturally work together.

To become fluent, learners must not only understand the meaning of a word, but also understand its nuances, how to use it in conversation, how to pair it with other words, where it fits into natural word order, and how it is used in grammar structures. No textbook could ever be written to teach all of this explicitly. When used properly, a textbook introduces the language and provides the basic meanings, while graded readers consolidate, strengthen, and deepen understanding.

Without graded readers, learners would have to study dictionaries, textbooks, sample dialogs, and simple conversations until they have randomly encountered enough Chinese for it to enter their comfort zones. With proper use of graded readers, learners can tackle this issue and develop greater fluency now, at their current levels, instead of waiting until some period in the distant future. With a stronger foundation and greater confidence at their current levels, learners are encouraged and motivated to continue their Chinese studies to even greater heights. Plus, they'll quickly learn that reading Chinese is fun!

About Mandarin Companion

Mandarin Companion was started by Jared Turner and John Pasden who met one fateful day on a bus in Shanghai when the only remaining seat left them sitting next to each other. A year later, Jared had greatly improved his Chinese using extensive reading but was frustrated at the lack of suitable reading materials. He approached John with the prospect of creating their own series. Having worked in Chinese education for nearly a decade, John was intrigued with the idea and thus began the Mandarin Companion series.

John majored in Japanese in college, but started learning Mandarin and later moved to China where his learning accelerated. After developing language proficiency, he was admitted into an all-Chinese masters program in applied linguistics at East China Normal University in Shanghai. Throughout his learning process, John developed an open mind to different learning styles and a tendency to challenge conventional wisdom in the field of teaching Chinese. He has since worked at ChinesePod as academic director and host, and opened his own consultancy, AllSet Learning, in Shanghai to help individuals acquire Chinese language proficiency. He lives in Shanghai with his wife and children.

After graduate school and with no Chinese language skills, Jared decided to move to China with his young family in search of career opportunities. Later while working on an investment project, Jared learned about extensive reading and decided that if it was as effective as it claimed to be, it could help him learn Chinese. In three months, he read 10 Chinese graded readers and his language ability quickly improved from speaking words and phrases to a conversational level. Jared has an MBA from Purdue University and a bachelor in Economics from the University of Utah. He lives in Shanghai with his wife and children.

Credits

Original Author: John Pasden

Story Authors: John Pasden, Jared Turner

Editor-in-Chief: John Pasden

Content Editor: Chen Shishuang

Editors: Li Jiong, Ma Lihua

Illustrator: Hu Sheng

Producer: Jared Turner

Acknowledgments

We are grateful to Ma Lihua, Li Jiong, Song Shen, Tan Rong, Chen Shishuang, and the entire team at AllSet Learning for working on this project and contributing the perfect mix of talent to produce this series.

Special thanks to Wang Hui and her 7th grade Chinese dual immersion class at Adele C. Young Intermediate School for being our test readers: AJ Bushnell, Brandon Murray, Colin Grunander, Emma Page, Isaak Diehl, Jackson Faerber, Jason Lee, Kyden Cefalo, Max Norton, Maxwell Isaacson, Olivia Barker, and Xavier Putnam. Also thanks to Jake Liu, Paris Yamamoto, and Rory O'Neill for being our test readers.

Table of Contents

Story Adaptation Notes

Any learner that has managed to learn 150 Chinese characters knows it is not an easy task, and the prospect of reading a real text in Chinese seems discouragingly far-off. Typically textbook dialogs are the only reading material available for years on end. That's why being able to read an actual story with only 150 Chinese characters is a very big deal, and a huge help to the fluency development of early-stage learners.

The stories told at this 150-character Breakthrough Level are special, however. Nouns, verbs, and adjectives at this level are in short supply, and the stories revolve around the limited vocabulary by necessity. This is why Breakthrough Level stories are not adaptations of western classics. They are original stories co-written by John Pasden and Jared Turner, specifically designed to be engaging to readers despite the limitations.

This story also ties into the larger "Mandarin Companion Universe." You'll read about how young Gao Ming (Sherlock Holmes) got his start and, as an added bonus, the name he goes by in this story is even a very common boy's nickname used in traditional Chinese stories. If you're curious how things turn out for him, you'll definitely want to prepare to read *The Case of the Red-Headed League*, a Mandarin Companion Level 1 story. For those who can read this book at an enjoyable pace, you are already well on your way towards progressing to the Level 1 stories.

Cast of Characters

小明
(Xiǎo Míng)

小天
(Xiǎo Tiān)

欢欢
(Huānhuān)

大头
(Dàtóu)

小月
(Xiǎo Yuè)

小四
(Xiǎosì)

方学东
(Fāng Xuédōng)

方太太
(Fāng Tàitai)

马太太
(Mǎ Tàitai)

Locations

上海 (Shànghǎi)

Known as "The Paris of the East, the New York of the West", early 1900's Shanghai was a bustling center of commerce and western influence in pre-modern China. Today it is the center of business in modern day China.

Story 1: 书

— Chapter 1 —
一本书

"欢欢，这本书是你的吗?"小天 问。

小天 是小明 的哥哥。小天、小明
和欢欢 是朋友，有时候 会一起 去上学。

欢欢 说:"不是我的书，是我朋友
的。我昨天去他家，看到 了这本书。我
朋友 说我可以看几天。"

小天 看了看书的名字，说:"我没
听说 过这本书。是谁写的?"

---

1 哥哥 (gēge) *n.* older brother
2 朋友 (péngyou) *n.* friend
3 有时候 (yǒu shíhou) *phrase* sometimes
4 一起 (yīqǐ) *adv.* together
5 上学 (shàngxué) *vo.* to start school, to go to school
6 家 (jiā) *n.* home
7 看到 (kàndào) *vc.* to see
8 名字 (míngzi) *n.* name
9 听说 (tīngshuō) *v.* to hear tell, to hear said (that)

小明 说:"是一个很有名的 外国人
　　　　　　　　　10
写的，很好看。"
　　　　11

听到 小天 和欢欢 说话，大头 走了过来
12　　　　　　　13　　　　　　　14
说:"什么书这么 好看? 拿来 给我看看!"
　　　　15　　11　　16　　　17

"不。"欢欢 马上走开 了。
　　　　　　　18

---

10 有名的 (yǒumíng de) *adj.* famous
11 好看 (hǎokàn) *adj.* good-looking
12 听到 (tīngdào) *vc.* to hear
13 说话 (shuōhuà) *vo.* to speak
  (words), to talk

14 走了过来 (zǒu le guòlai) *phrase*
  walked over
15 这么 (zhème) *adv.* so…
16 拿来 (nálái) *vc.* to fetch
17 看看 (kànkan) *v.* to take a look
18 走开 (zǒukāi) *vc.* to go away

"你太小气了！"大头天天对欢欢
很不好。

"这是什么书？我要看一下！"大头
说。

"不，你不要过来，你不要过来。我
要叫老师了！"欢欢生气地大叫。

"那你去叫，我看老师能做什么。你
去叫！"大头笑了。大头的爸爸也是这
里的老师。

欢欢不说话，生气地看大头。

"你小心一点，谁知道这本书明天
会在谁手上。"大头说。

---

19 小气 (xiǎoqì) *adj.* stingy, petty
20 天天 (tiāntiān) *adv.* every day
21 一下 (yīxià) *adv.* briefly, for a second
22 过来 (guòlai) *vc.* to come over
23 叫 (jiào) *v.* to call, to be called
24 生气地 (shēngqì de) *phrase* angrily

25 大叫 (dà jiào) *v.* to call out loudly
26 笑 (xiào) *v.* to laugh, to smile
27 小心一点 (xiǎoxīn yīdiǎn) *phrase* to be (more) careful
28 手上 (shǒushang) *phrase* in one's hand(s)

— Chapter 2 —
书不见了

第二天，欢欢 的书不见了。
<u>29</u>   <u>30</u>

"谁拿 了我的书？你看见 我的书了
<u>31</u>   <u>32</u>

吗？"他问每一个学生。

"怎么了，欢欢，是什么书？"小明
<u>33</u>

问。

"是我朋友 的书，我明天要给他的
<u>2</u>

……要是 他知道书不见了，会很生气
<u>34</u>   <u>30</u>   <u>35</u>

的。"

"今天你看到 你的书了吗？"小明
<u>7</u>

---

29 第二天 (dì-èr tiān) *phrase* the next
   day, the second day
30 不见了 (bùjiàn le) *phrase*
   disappeared
31 拿 (ná) *v.* to get, to hold
32 看见 (kànjian) *vc.* to see

33 怎么了 (zěnme le) *phrase* what
   happened, what's the matter
34 要是 (yàoshi) *conj.* if
35 生气 (shēngqì) *vo., adj.* to get angry;
   angry

问。

"对，今天早上 我还 看到 这本书……小明，大头 昨天要看我的书，我没给他。他说了很多不好听 的话，他还说，要我小心一点。"欢欢 生气地 说。

小明 想了想，问："你觉得是大头拿 的?"

"不是他，会是谁? 我要去跟老师说!"欢欢 说。

"不要去，欢欢。"小明 说。

"我知道是他! 是他拿 了我的书!"欢欢 说。

---

36 早上 (zǎoshang) *tn.* morning
37 还 (hái) *adv.* still
38 不好听 (bù hǎotīng) *phrase* unpleasant-sounding

39 想了想 (xiǎng le xiǎng) *phrase* thought about it for a second

"欢欢，我知道大头 对你很不好，你

很不开心。可是，你不能说书是大头 拿
　　　　40　　　41　　　　　　　　31

的，跟老师说了也没有用。"
　　　　　　　　　42

"那，你说怎么办？"
　　　　　43

"他在外面，我去问问他。"小明 走
　　　　44

40 不开心 (bù kāixīn) *phrase* not
　 happy, to be unhappy
41 可是 (kěshì) *conj.* but
42 没有用 (méiyǒu yòng) *phrase* to be
　 of no use

43 怎么办 (zěnme bàn) *phrase* what is
　 one to do
44 外面 (wàimian) *n.* outside

7

了出去。

— Chapter 3 —
大头拿的？

大头 和小月 在外面 说话。

"大头，欢欢 的书不见了，你知道

吗?"小明 问。

"不会吧?"大头 笑 了。"我昨天跟他

说了，要小心一点。你看，我说对了！"

说完， 他还 在笑。

"书是不是你拿 的?"小明 问。

"不是我拿 的， 走开！"大头 生气

了。

"大头，你不要这么 生气。要是 你

---

45 说对了 (shuō duì le) *phrase* to get it
right

46 说完 (shuō wán) *vc.* to finish
speaking

没拿 的话，我们可以看一下 你这里的
书吗？"小明 说。

"看我这里的书？你觉得你是谁？！"
大头 大叫。好几个人 走过来 看他们，
欢欢 也出来 了。

"大头，要是 你没拿，他们看一下
可以吧。"小月 说。

47 走过来 (zǒu guòlai) vc. to walk over　48 出来 (chūlai) vc. to come out

大头听了有一点不开心。他不说话，
也不看小明和欢欢。过了一会儿，他看
了看小月，说："好，你们都过来。"

"大家都看见了吧，我这里什么也
没有。"大头说。

---

49 听 (tīng) *v.* to listen (to)

50 有一点 (yǒu yīdiǎn) *phrase* to be a
little (too)

51 一会儿 (yīhuìr) *tn.* a little while

52 大家 (dàjiā) *n.* everyone

"欢欢，大头 没有拿 你的书。你的
书是不是还 在家 里？"小明 问。

"对，欢欢，你今天回家 看看。"大家
也这样 说。

"我们家 有那么 多书，谁会拿 他的
书！"大头 跟大家 说。

"不可能，书不在我家！是大头 拿
的。"欢欢 大叫。

"你再 说，我……"大头 又 生气 了。

"欢欢，昨天你回家 的时候，我看见
书在你这里。"小天 说。"你还 说，要拿
回家 看完。"

---

53 这样 (zhèyàng) *pr.* like this
54 那么 (nàme) *adv.* so…
55 不可能 (bù kěnéng) *phrase*
impossible (to)
56 再 (zài) *adv.* again (in the future)

57 又 (yòu) *adv.* again, and also
58 的时候 (de shíhou) *phrase* when…

欢欢 想了想，不说话 了。

— Chapter 4 —
是他

小月 说：“昨天大头 的书都没有拿
回家，一个老师去跟他爸爸说了，他爸
爸很生气。可是 也没有办法，他爸爸去
了我家。昨天，大头 看的书、用的本子，
都是我的。”

“要是 大头 昨天没有拿 书回家，也
不可能 拿 你的书。”小明 看看 大头，又
看看 欢欢，说：“欢欢，大头 昨天没有
拿 你的书。书还 在你家，对不对？”

欢欢 还是 不说话。过了一会儿，他

---

59 办法 (bànfǎ) *n.* way (of doing），
solution

60 本子 (běnzi) *n.* notebook
61 还是 (háishi) *conj., adv.* still

说:"是的，书还 在我家。这本书太好看
了，要是 我也有一本多好。可是 我没钱
……要是 大家 都觉得是大头 拿 了我的
书……"

小明 说:"要是 大家 都觉得是大头
拿 了你的书，你可以去跟大头 的爸爸

62 多好 (duō hǎo) *phrase* so great   63 钱 (qián) *n.* money

说，大头 的爸爸会给你书钱，这样 你也可以有一本书。我知道了。"

大头 听 了，大叫："我说了不是我拿 的书！现在大家 都知道了吧。"

大头 又 对欢欢 说："你说我拿 了你的书，你以后 小心一点 !"

欢欢 不说话。小月 看了看欢欢，看了看大头，不知道说什么。

大头 生气地 走了。

64 以后 (yǐhòu) *adv.* after; later, in the future

Story 2: 火

— Chapter 5 —
起火了

方学东 的家 很小。在这里，每个
人的家 都很小，家 里没有做饭 的地方。
几家人 在一个地方 做饭。方学东 和太太
每天也在这里做饭。小明 一家人 也在
这里。

方学东 有一个儿子，还没上学，叫
小四。有时候，小明 会跟小四 一起 玩。

方学东 每天都很早起来 做饭。他没
办法，这里的人太多，地方 太小。要是

---

65 做饭 (zuò fàn) *vo.* to cook a meal
66 地方 (dìfang) *n.* place
67 几家人 (jǐ jiā rén) *phrase* several families (of people)
68 太太 (tàitai) *n.* wife, lady, Mrs.

69 一家人 (yī jiā rén) *phrase* the whole family
70 儿子 (érzi) *n.* son
71 起来 (qǐlai) *vc.* to get up; upward

18

六点以后 起来，做饭 的地方 会有很多
　　　　64　　71　　　65　　　　66
人。

　　一天早上 五点多，方学东 在门边
　　　　　　36　　　　　　　　　　72
对太太 大叫："不好了，起火 了！"
　68　　25　　　　73　　　74

　　"我的天！"方太太 走出来， 看到
　　　　　　　　　　　　75　　　7

---

72 门边 (mén biān) *phrase* by the door
73 不好了 (bù hǎo le) *phrase* (this is)
　　not good!

74 起火 (qǐhuǒ) *vo.* to catch fire/to
　　cook/to get angry
75 走出来 (zǒu chūlai) *vc.* to walk out
　　(from)

门边 的东西 起火 了，马上又 走进去。"我
去拿 水！"

方太太用了很多水，火一下子 没
了。

"我在做早饭，开门 的时候 看到
起火 了。"方学东 对太太 说，"还好，火
不大。"

76 东西 (dōngxi) *n.* thing(s), stuff
77 进去 (jìnqu) *vc.* to go in
78 一下子 (yīxiàzi) *adv.* all of a sudden; all at once
79 开门 (kāimén) *vo.* to open the door
80 还好 (hái hǎo) *phrase* not bad; tolerable; fortunately

— Chapter 6 —
是不是马太太？

第二天，在这里的人都听说了方学东家早上起火了。

"怎么会起火？"马太太问方学东。

"我们也不知道，我出来的时候，没有看到人。"方学东说。

"五点多太早了，谁会那么早起来，在你家门边点火？"一个女人说。

"好了好了，大家都要小心一点，这么多人在这里。"一个男人说。"要是早上四点的时候这里起火，大家都还

---

81 怎么会 (zěnme huì) *phrase* how could

82 点火 (diǎnhuǒ) *vo.* to light a fire

没起来，那……"
<u>71</u>

　　<u>大家</u> 走了以后，<u>方学东</u> 想了想，对
　　<u>52</u>　　　<u>64</u>　　　　　　　<u>39</u>

<u>太太</u> 说："上个星期，<u>马太太</u> 说，我家
<u>68</u>　　　　　<u>83</u>　　　<u>68</u>　　　<u>6</u>

的<u>东西</u> 太多了，我们用了<u>大家</u> 的<u>地方</u>，
　<u>76</u>　　　　　　　　　<u>52</u>　　<u>66</u>

要我们<u>拿进去</u>。"
　　　<u>84</u>

---

83 星期 (xīngqī) *n.* week　　　　84 拿进去 (ná jìnqu) *vc.* to take in(side)

"老公，你觉得是马太太 点的火？
不可能 吧……"方太太说。

方学东 看看 马太太 家 的大门，没
说话。

— Chapter 7 —
又起火了

那天 以后，方学东 家 大门的一边
还是 有很多东西，他们没有拿进去。

过了一个星期，方学东 早上 五点
多开门 出去拿 东西，看到 外面 又 起火
了。

"又 起火 了！"方学东 对太太 大叫。
方太太听到 以后，马上起来 了。

"老公，怎么 又 起火 了？"方太太也
走了出来。

"我怎么 知道？"方学东 说。

---

86 那天 (nà tiān) *tn.* that day　　　88 怎么 (zěnme) *adv.* how
87 一边 (yībiān) *n.* one side

他马上拿 水出来，火一下子 没了。
　　　　 31　　　 48　　　　 78

这时候，马太太 走了出来："你看，
89　　　　 68　　　 48

我说的吧，你家 门边 的东西 太多了。"
　　　　　　 6　 72　　 76

方学东 也不说话，看起来 很生气。
　　　　　 13　　　 90　　 35

方太太说："你家 门边 也有很多
　　　　　　 6　 72

东西，不是吗？"
76

---

89 这时候 (zhè shíhou) *phrase* at this
time

90 看起来 (kàn qǐlai) *vc.* to look…

马太太听了很生气，没说什么。

Chapter 8
点火的人

第二天，大人们都知道了方学东 家
又 起火 了。小明 也听说 了。

小明 想："我要知道点火 的人是
谁。"

小明 想了想，知道了怎么 做。

星期六 早上，小明 起得很早，还
不到五点。他出门 的时候，家里人 都
不知道。

小明 来到方学东 家 西面的地方，
太早了，还 看不见一个人。

---

91 星期六 (Xīngqīliù) *tn.* Saturday
92 出门 (chūmén) *vo.* to go out the
  door, to go outside

93 家里人 (jiālǐ rén) *n.* family members

一个小时以后，一个人出来了。

这个人看起来很开心，不知道在做什么。

小明又看了看。

"是小四！这么早，小四在做什么？是小四点的火吗？他还那么小。"小明想。

小明看到他手里有一个东西，小四看起来很开心。

"小四，回家去。"小明叫了一下。可是，小四没听到。

"小四……"小明又叫了一下。小四听到小明叫他，马上进去了。

---

94 开心 (kāixīn) *adj.* happy　　　95 手里 (shǒu lǐ) *phrase* in one's hand

小四 进去 以后，门边 的东西 起火
了。

　　"是小四！可是，小四 怎么会 点火？
他还 那么 小。"小明 想。

　　小四 进去 以后，小明 看到 起火 了。
火有一点 大，小明 到方学东 家 门边，

29

大叫：“起火了！”

方学东马上拿水出来，火一下子没了。

“小明，怎么是你？今天你这么早来这里？”方学东问。

“我想知道是谁点火的。”小明说。

“那，你看到点火的人了吗？”方学东问。

“看到了，是小四。”小明说。

“怎么可能……”方学东有一点儿生气，看看家里：“小四，你出来。”

小四走了出来，方太太也起来了。

96 可能 (kěnéng) *adv.; aux* maybe, possibly; possible

"儿子，你玩火 了吗？"

小四 在方太太后面，不说话，也不
看方学东。

"小四，我看到 你了。"小明 说。

小明 说完，方学东 看起来 很生气！

方学东 问小四：“是你吗？”

97 玩火 (wán huǒ) *vo.* to play with fire

小四 不说话。
13

方学东 又 问："是你吗？ 是你吗？
57
说！"

小四 小心地 说："我……我觉得火
98
好玩。"
99

方学东 很生气，说："家 里有很多
35   6
东西，你都可以玩，可是，你不能玩火！
76   41   97
要是 起火 了怎么办？怎么办？你回家！"
34 74   43   43   6

小四 不说话，进去 了。
13   77

"谢谢你，小明。"方太太对小明。

"不用谢。"
100

---

98 小心地 (xiǎoxīn de) *phrase* carefully
99 好玩 (hǎowán) *adj.* fun

100 不用谢 (bùyòng xiè) *phrase* You're
welcome (lit. "no need to thank")

Story 3: 花

— Chapter 9 —
谁送的花？

中饭 的时候，小月 和小明 说：“小明，

在这一个月，有人送我花。可是，我不

知道这个人是谁。”

“你没看到 送花的人？”小明 问。

“没有，我早上 出门 的时候，在大

门外面 看到 了花。”小月 说。

“这个人每天都送吗？”

“一个星期 会送三四次。”小月 说。“花

上面 有我的 名字，没有送花的人的

名字。”

---

101 中饭 (zhōngfàn) *n.* lunch

102 上面 (shàngmian) *n.* on, on top,
above

"这个人喜欢你，可是，又怕你知
道。"小明 对小月 笑 了。

"我想知道他是谁。小明，你有办法
吗？"小月 问。

---

103 喜欢 (xǐhuan) *v.* to like   104 怕 (pà) *v.* to be afraid (of)

"我有办法。"

第二天 早上，小明 起得很早。他来
到了小月 家 外面 的一个地方。过了一
个多小时，他看到 几个人 走过去。可是，
没看到 送花的人。

那个星期，小明 每天都早起，可是，
他一次 也没看到 有人来送花。小月 也
几天都没看到 花。

"那个人可能 不会再 送了吧。"小明
对小月 说。

第二个星期，小明 不去小月 家 了。

105 过去 (guòqu) vc. to go over   107 一次 (yīcì) phrase one time
106 早起 (zǎoqǐ) phrase to get up early

— Chapter 10 —
有办法了

可是，那个星期的第一天，小月又在家门边看到了花。

"怎么会这样？"中饭的时候，小月问小明，"这个人怎么会知道你今天不来？"

"这个人可能知道我在那儿。他看得见我，可是，我看不见他。"

"我有一点怕。小明，我们去跟老师说吧。"

"不能跟老师说。老师会说很多

---

108 第一天 (dì-yī tiān) *phrase* the first
day

没有用 的话。"小明 笑 了一下，"小月，
你不用怕，我有办法。"

三天以后，小月 对小明 说："小明，
那个人又 来送花了。这几天每天都送。"

"我知道。"小明 说完，笑 了。

小月 问，"你这几天早上 都没来，你
怎么 知道？"

"我知道，可是，我还 不能说。"小明
说。

"你在做什么？知道了也不跟我说？"
小月 听起来 有一点 生气。

小明 说："不要怕，听 我的。下个
星期一，花你都拿 过来。"

"我不要……"

"你怕 什么？"小明 问。

"要是 我这样 做，大家 都知道有人
送我花了，老师也会知道。"

"可是，要是 你不这样 做，我也没
办法 跟你说送花的人是谁了。"

"好吧，我听 你的。"小月 说。

— Chapter 11 —
打起来了！

第三个星期一 早上，大家 都看到
了小月 的花。很多女生都在跟她说话。

"小月，花很好看！谁送的?"

"小月，你有男朋友 了?"

"小月，他是不是……"

大头 看大家 又 说又 笑，很生气。

他 走 到 外面， 大叫："小天，你
过来 !"

小天 和 几个男生在玩，没听到 大头
叫 他。

---

111 男朋友 (nánpéngyou) *n.*
boyfriend

大头 生气地 走过去，要拿 手里 的
书去打小天。

"大头，你做什么？"小天 叫 了 起来。"去
叫 小明。"小天 对一个男生说。

"大头，你做什么？不可以打人！"
小月 走过来，对大头 说。

"大头，你为什么打人？"小月 生气地
问。

"小天 ……"大头 没说完，他 看看
小天，又 看看 小月。

"小天 怎么了？"小月 问。

大头 说："小月，我……你知道早上
有人去你家 送花，对吧？那个人……是
我。"

小月 不知道说什么了。

"我怕 你……"大头 没说完。

"你怕 小月 不喜欢 你？"小天 说。

大头 不说话，点点头。

Chapter 12
他说了

小月 问："你怕 我不喜欢 你，可是，
你为什么要打小天？"

"小天 也喜欢 你！"大头 生气地 说，"上
个星期，他也去你家 送花了。我看到 了！
可是，他是跟我学的！你是我 女朋友！
不是小天 的 女朋友！"

小月 有一点 生气："谁说我是你
女朋友？ 我不是你 女朋友！我也不是
小天 的 女朋友！"

"小月 不要生气，不要生气。"小天
对小月 笑 笑。

小天 又 对大头 说:"上个星期, 我去
小月 家 送花了。可是, 我不喜欢 小月。"

大头 说:"怎么 可能? 要是 你不喜欢
她, 你怎么会 天天 去送花?"

"这是小明 的办法。"小天 说。

小明 也走过来 了。

小明 说:"上上个 星期,我们要知道谁是送花的人。我每天都早起 去小月家。可是,送花的人一个星期 都没来。"

小月 说:"你知道为什么他不去送花了。送花的人看见 了你。"

大头 问小明:"我看到 你送花了,可是,小天 为什么也去送花?"

小天 看看 小月 说:"小明 知道,要是还 有一个男生也送花,喜欢 小月 的人会不开心。小明 说对了。"

大头 不说话 了。

他们四个人都不说话 了。

113 上上个 (shàng-shàng ge) *phrase*
the one before last

— Chapter 13 —
知道了

过了一会儿，小明 问小天："哥哥，
你还好 吗?"

小天 看看 小明 说:"我还好。"

大头 不说话。

小明 看看 大头，又 看看 小月，对
小月 说:"对不起，小月。这个办法 对
你不太好，可是，你知道了送花的人是
谁。"

小月 想了想，没说话。

大头 又 看看 小月 说:"对不起,小月,
我……我不送花了。"

114 对不起 (duìbuqǐ) *phrase* I'm sorry

小月 说:"你不是我男朋友,知道

吗?"

大头 说:"我知道了。"

"可是 ……你是第一个给我送花的

人。"

大头 不知道说什么,看了看小月。

小月 又 说："我喜欢 花。下次送花，
我要知道是谁送的。"

说完，小月 笑 了笑，走了。

Key Words 关键词 (Guānjiàncí)

1. 哥哥 (gēge) *n.* older brother
2. 朋友 (péngyou) *n.* friend
3. 有时候 (yǒu shíhou) *phrase* sometimes
4. 一起 (yìqǐ) *adv.* together
5. 上学 (shàngxué) *vo.* to start school, to go to school
6. 家 (jiā) *n.* home
7. 看到 (kàndào) *vc.* to see
8. 名字 (míngzi) *n.* name
9. 听说 (tīngshuō) *v.* to hear tell, to hear said (that)
10. 有名的 (yǒumíng de) *adj.* famous
11. 好看 (hǎokàn) *adj.* good-looking
12. 听到 (tīngdào) *vc.* to hear
13. 说话 (shuōhuà) *vo.* to speak (words), to talk
14. 走了过来 (zǒu le guòlai) *phrase* walked over
15. 这么 (zhème) *adv.* so…
16. 拿来 (nálái) *vc.* to fetch
17. 看看 (kànkan) *v.* to take a look
18. 走开 (zǒukāi) *vc.* to go away
19. 小气 (xiǎoqì) *adj.* stingy, petty
20. 天天 (tiāntiān) *adv.* every day
21. 一下 (yīxià) *adv.* briefly, for a second
22. 过来 (guòlai) *vc.* to come over
23. 叫 (jiào) *v.* to call, to be called
24. 生气地 (shēngqì de) *phrase* angrily
25. 大叫 (dà jiào) *v.* to call out loudly
26. 笑 (xiào) *v.* to laugh, to smile
27. 小心一点 (xiǎoxīn yīdiǎn) *phrase* to be (more) careful
28. 手上 (shǒushang) *phrase* in one's hand(s)
29. 第二天 (dì-èr tiān) *phrase* the next day, the second day
30. 不见了 (bùjiàn le) *phrase* disappeared

Springdale Public Library
405 S. Pleasant
Springdale, AR 72764

31. 拿 (ná) *v.* to get, to hold

32. 看见 (kànjian) *vc.* to see

33. 怎么了 (zěnme le) *phrase* what happened, what's the matter

34. 要是 (yàoshi) *conj.* if

35. 生气 (shēngqì) *vo., adj.* to get angry; angry

36. 早上 (zǎoshang) *tn.* morning

37. 还 (hái) *adv.* still

38. 不好听 (bù hǎotīng) *phrase* unpleasant-sounding

39. 想了想 (xiǎng le xiǎng) *phrase* thought about it for a second

40. 不开心 (bù kāixīn) *phrase* not happy, to be unhappy

41. 可是 (kěshì) *conj.* but

42. 没有用 (méiyǒu yòng) *phrase* to be of no use

43. 怎么办 (zěnme bàn) *phrase* what is one to do

44. 外面 (wàimian) *n.* outside

45. 说对了 (shuō duì le) *phrase* to get it right

46. 说完 (shuō wán) *vc.* to finish speaking

47. 走过来 (zǒu guòlai) *vc.* to walk over

48. 出来 (chūlai) *vc.* to come out

49. 听 (tīng) *v.* to listen (to)

50. 有一点 (yǒu yīdiǎn) *phrase* to be a little (too)

51. 一会儿 (yīhuìr) *tn.* a little while

52. 大家 (dàjiā) *n.* everyone

53. 这样 (zhèyàng) *pr.* like this

54. 那么 (nàme) *adv.* so...

55. 不可能 (bù kěnéng) *phrase* impossible (to)

56. 再 (zài) *adv.* again (in the future)

57. 又 (yòu) *adv.* again, and also

58. 的时候 (de shíhou) *phrase* when...

59. 办法 (bànfǎ) *n.* way (of doing), solution

60. 本子 (běnzi) *n.* notebook

61. 还是 (háishi) *conj., adv.* still

62. 多好 (duō hǎo) *phrase* so great

63. 钱 (qián) *n.* money

64. 以后 (yǐhòu) *adv.* after; later, in the future

65. 做饭 (zuò fàn) *vo.* to cook a meal

66. 地方 (dìfang) *n.* place

67. 几家人 (jǐ jiā rén) *phrase* several families (of people)

68. 太太 (tàitai) *n.* wife, lady, Mrs.

69. 一家人 (yī jiā rén) *phrase* the whole family

70. 儿子 (érzi) *n.* son

71. 起来 (qǐlai) *vc.* to get up; upward

72. 门边 (mén biān) *phrase* by the door

73. 不好了 (bù hǎo le) *phrase* (this is) not good!

74. 起火 (qǐhuǒ) *vo.* to catch fire/to cook/to get angry

75. 走出来 (zǒu chūlai) *vc.* to walk out (from)

76. 东西 (dōngxi) *n.* thing(s), stuff

77. 进去 (jìnqu) *vc.* to go in

78. 一下子 (yīxiàzi) *adv.* all of a sudden; all at once

79. 开门 (kāimén) *vo.* to open the door

80. 还好 (hái hǎo) *phrase* not bad; tolerable; fortunately

81. 怎么会 (zěnme huì) *phrase* how could

82. 点火 (diǎnhuǒ) *vo.* to light a fire

83. 星期 (xīngqī) *n.* week

84. 拿进去 (ná jìnqu) *vc.* to take in(side)

85. 老公 (lǎogōng) *n.* husband

86. 那天 (nà tiān) *tn.* that day

87. 一边 (yībiān) *n.* one side

88. 怎么 (zěnme) *adv.* how

89. 这时候 (zhè shíhou) *phrase* at this time

90. 看起来 (kàn qǐlai) *vc.* to look…

91. 星期六 (Xīngqīliù) *tn.* Saturday

92. 出门 (chūmén) *vo.* to go out the door, to go outside

93. 家里人 (jiālǐ rén) *n.* family members

94. 开心 (kāixīn) *adj.* happy

95. 手里 (shǒu lǐ) *phrase* in one's hand

96. 可能 (kěnéng) *adv.; aux* maybe, possibly; possible

97. 玩火 (wán huǒ) *vo.* to play with fire

98. 小心地 (xiǎoxīn de) *phrase* carefully

99. 好玩 (hǎowán) *adj.* fun

100. 不用谢 (bùyòng xiè) *phrase* You're welcome (lit. "no need to thank")

101. 中饭 (zhōngfàn) *n.* lunch

102. 上面 (shàngmian) *n.* on, on top, above

103. 喜欢 (xǐhuan) *v.* to like

104. 怕 (pà) *v.* to be afraid (of)

105. 过去 (guòqu) *vc.* to go over

106. 早起 (zǎoqǐ) *phrase* to get up early

107. 一次 (yīcì) *phrase* one time

108. 第一天 (dì-yī tiān) *phrase* the first day

109. 听起来 (tīng qǐlai) *vc.* to sound...

110. 星期一 (Xīngqīyī) *tn.* Monday

111. 男朋友 (nánpéngyou) *n.* boyfriend

112. 女朋友 (nǚpéngyou) *n.* girlfriend

113. 上上个 (shàng-shàng ge) *phrase* the one before last

114. 对不起 (duìbuqǐ) *phrase* I'm sorry

Part of Speech Key

adj. Adjective

adv. Adverb

aux. Auxiliary Verb

conj. Conjunction

cov. Coverb

mw. Measure word

n. Noun

on. Onomatopoeia

part. Particle

prep. Preposition

pr. Pronoun

pn. Proper noun

tn. Time Noun

v. Verb

vc. Verb plus complement

vo. Verb plus object

Discussion Questions
讨论问题 (Tǎolùn Wèntí)

Chapter 1 一本书

1. 那本书是谁的?
2. 欢欢和大头是好朋友吗？为什么?
3. 你喜欢看什么样的书?

Chapter 2 书不见了

1. 欢欢为什么说大头拿了他的书?
2. 你觉得是大头拿了欢欢的书吗？为什么?
3. 如果别人拿了你的书，你会怎么做?

Chapter 3 大头拿的?

1. 大头为什么笑了?
2. 小明为什么说大头没有拿欢欢的书?
3. 要是你是大头，你会怎么做?

Chapter 4 是他

1. 欢欢为什么对大家说大头拿了他的书?
2. 谁说的话很有用?
3. 你觉得欢欢怎么样？为什么?

Chapter 5 起火了

1. 方学东为什么每天要很早起来做饭?
2. 你每天几点起来？在哪里做饭?
3. 小时候你玩过火吗?

Chapter 6 是不是马太太?

1. 为什么大家不知道怎么会起火了?
2. 马太太对方学东说了什么?
3. 你觉得方学东会怎么做?

Chapter 7 又起火了

1. 方学东为什么很生气?
2. 马太太为什么起得那么早?
3. 马太太喜欢方学东和方太太吗? 为什么?

Chapter 8 点火的人

1. 星期六早上，小明为什么起得很早?
2. 你觉得小四为什么要玩火?
3. 你玩过火吗? 好玩吗?

Chapter 9 谁送的花?

1. 小月为什么不知道送花的人是谁?
2. 送花的人为什么不写自己的名字?
3. 有人送过你花吗? 是谁?

Chapter 10 有办法了

1. 小月为什么有点怕?
2. 你有办法知道送花的人是谁吗?
3. 你给谁送过花? 你给老师送过花吗?

Chapter 11 打起来了！

1. 小月有男朋友吗？
2. 大头为什么给小月送花？
3. 大家为什么喜欢送花？

Chapter 12 他说了

1. 大头为什么要打小天？
2. 小天为什么送花给小月？
3. 小明的办法好吗？

Chapter 13 知道了

1. 小月喜欢大头吗？
2. 小天喜欢小月吗？
3. 你觉得大头还会给小月送花吗？

Appendix A:
Character Comparison Reference

This appendix is designed to help Chinese teachers and learners use the Mandarin Companion graded readers as a companion to the most popular university textbooks and the HSK word lists.

The tables below compare the characters and vocabulary used in other study materials with those found in this Mandarin Companion graded reader. The tables below will display the exact characters and vocabulary used in this book and not covered by these sources. A learner who has studied these textbooks will likely find it easier to read this graded reader by focusing on these characters and words.

Integrated Chinese Level 1, Part 1 (3rd Ed.)

Words and characters in this story not covered by these textbooks:

Character	Pinyin	Word(s)	Pinyin
欢	huān	欢欢 喜欢	Huānhuān xǐhuan
哥	gē	哥哥	gēge
起	qǐ	一起 起火 起来 看起来 起 早起 对不起	yīqǐ qǐhuǒ qǐlái kànqǐlái qǐ zǎoqǐ duìbuqǐ
走	zǒu	走 走开 走过 走进	zǒu zǒukāi zǒuguò zǒujìn
拿	ná	拿 拿来	ná nálái
能	néng	能 可能	néng kěnéng

Character	Pinyin	Word(s)	Pinyin
做	zuò	做 做饭	zuò zuòfàn
笑	xiào	笑	xiào
爸	bà	爸爸	bàba
想	xiǎng	想	xiǎng
觉	jiào	觉得	juéde
办	bàn	怎么办 办法	zěnmebàn bànfǎ
现	xiàn	现在	xiànzài
后	Hòu	以后 后面	yǐhòu hòumiàn
玩	wán	玩 玩火 好玩	wán wánhuǒ hǎowán
边	biān	门边 一边	mén-biān yībiān
进	jìn	走进 进去	zǒujìn jìnqù
花	huā	花	huā
送	sòng	送 送花	sòng sònghuā
喜	xǐ	喜欢	xǐhuan
怕	pà	怕	pà
打	dǎ	打 打人	dǎ dǎ rén

New Practical Chinese Reader, Book 1 (1st Ed.)

Words and characters in this story not covered by these textbooks:

Character	Pinyin	Word(s)	Pinyin
走	zǒu	走	zǒu

Character	Pinyin	Word(s)	Pinyin
		走开	zǒukāi
		走过	zǒuguò
		走进	zǒujìn
地	de	地	de
		地方	dìfang
笑	xiào	笑	xiào
手	shǒu	手上	shǒushang
		手里	shǒulǐ
早	zǎo	早上	zǎoshang
		早	zǎo
		早饭	zǎofàn
		早起	zǎoqǐ
完	wán	说完	shuōwán
		完	wán
又	yòu	又	yòu
后	Hòu	以后	yǐhòu
		后面	hòumiàn
火	huǒ	火	huǒ
		起火	qǐhuǒ
		点火	diǎnhuǒ
		玩火	wánhuǒ
门	mén	门边	mén biān
		开门	kāimén
		大门	dàmén
		出门	chūmén
边	biān	门边	mén biān
		一边	yībiān
花	huā	花	huā

Hanyu Shuiping Kaoshi (HSK) Levels 1-2

Words and characters in this story not covered by these levels:

Character	Pīnyīn	Word(s)	Pīnyīn
头	tóu	大头 点点头	Dàtou diǎndian tóu
拿	ná	拿 拿来	ná nálái
马	mǎ	马上 马太太	mǎshàng Mǎ Tàitai
地	de	地 地方	de dìfang
心	xīn	小心 开心	xiǎoxīn kāixīn
跟	gēn	跟	gēn
用	yòng	用 不用	yòng bùyòng
办	bàn	怎么办 办法	zěnme bàn bànfǎ
又	yòu	又	yòu
法	fǎ	办法	bànfǎ
方	fāng	方学东 地方 方	Fāng Xuédōng dìfang fāng
花	huā	花	huā
怕	pà	怕	pà

Appendix B: Grammar Point Index

For learners new to reading Chinese, an understanding of grammar points can be extremely helpful for learners and teachers. The following is a list of the most challenging grammar points used in this graded reader.

These grammar points correspond to the Common European Framework of Reference for Languages (CEFR) level A2 or above. The full list with explanations and examples of each grammar point can be found on the Chinese Grammar Wiki, the definitive source of information on Chinese grammar online.

CHAPTER 1	
Tag questions with "ma"	……是吗 / 对吗 / 好吗?
The "shi… de" construction for indicating purpose	是……的
Expressing "will" with "hui"	会 + Verb
Expressing location with "zai… shang / xia / li"	在 + Place + 上 / 下 / 里 / 旁边
Expressing "excessively" with "tai"	太 + Adj. + 了
Expressing "then…" with "name"	那么……
Expressing "be going to" with "yao"	Subj. + 要 + Verb (+ 了)
Expressing experiences with "guo"	Verb + 过
Verbing briefly with "yixia"	Verb + 一下
Reduplication of verbs	Verb + Verb
Expressing ability or possibility with "neng"	能 + Verb
Verbs preceded by "gei"	Subj. + 给 + Target + Verb + Obj.
Reduplication of measure words	MW + MW
Expressing "every" with "mei"	每 + Measure Word (+ Noun)
CHAPTER 2	
Expressing "would like to" with "xiang"	想 + Verb

Other Stories
from Mandarin Companion

Breakthrough Readers: 150 Characters

The Misadventures of Zhou Haisheng 《周海生》 by John Pasden, Jared Turner

My Teacher Is a Martian 《我的老师是火星人》 by John Pasden, Jared Turner

In Search of Hua Ma 《花马》 by John Pasden, Jared Turner

Just Friends? 《我们是朋友吗？》 by John Pasden, Jared Turner

Level 1 Readers: 300 Characters

The Secret Garden 《秘密花园》 by Frances Hodgson Burnett

The Sixty Year Dream 《六十年的梦》 by Washington Irving (based on *Rip Van Winkle*)

The Monkey's Paw 《猴爪》 by W. W. Jacobs

The Country of the Blind 《盲人国》 by H. G. Wells

Sherlock Holmes and the Case of the Curly-Haired Company 《卷发公司的案子》 by Sir Arthur Conan Doyle (based on *The Red Headed League*)

The Prince and the Pauper 《王子和穷孩子》 by Mark Twain

Emma 《安末》 by Jane Austen

The Ransom of Red Chief 《红猴的价格》 by O. Henry

Level 2 Readers: 450 Characters

Great Expectations: Part 1 《美好的前途（上）》 by Charles Dickens

Great Expectations: Part 2 《美好的前途（下）》 by Charles Dickens

Journey to the Center of the Earth 《地心游记》 by Jules Verne

Mandarin Companion is producing a growing library of graded readers for Chinese language learners.

Visit our website for the newest books available:

www.MandarinCompanion.com

CPSIA information can be obtained
at www.ICGtesting.com
Printed in the USA
LVHW011630180521
687784LV00003B/51